Spot-the-Differences Puzzle Fun

Fran Newman-D'Amico

DOVER PUBLICATIONS, INC.
Mineola, New York

Bibliographical Note

Spot-the-Differences Puzzle Fun is a new work, first published
by Dover Publications, Inc., in 2004.

International Standard Book Number
ISBN-13: 978-0-486-43841-2
ISBN-10: 0-486-43841-4

Manufactured in the United States by LSC Communications
43841412   2018
www.doverpublications.com

NOTE

In this little book, you will find entertaining pictures of underwater creatures, circus seals, a violinist, a football player, a mermaid and her friends, and many others. Each picture is shown twice. The two pictures seem the same, but look carefully and you will discover that the second picture has changes that make it different from the first. Find all of the differences and circle them. There is a Solutions section, which begins on page 58, but try doing all of the pages on your own before you check your answers. In addition, you can enjoy coloring the pictures after you have circled the differences. Have fun!

This underwater scene looks like the picture on the opposite page, doesn't it?

Now look at the picture. Find and circle the
4 things that are different.

5

Caitlin plays a princess in the school play.

There are 4 differences between this picture and the one opposite. Find and circle them.

Here is a picture of a spaceship taking off.

Find and circle the 5 things that have changed
in the picture.

9

The mother hen tells her chicks that
they will be eating soon.

Look again! Find and circle the 3 things that
are different in the picture.

11

Luke and Barney are racing to the bottom of the hill.

Find and circle the 5 things that make this
picture different from the one opposite.

13

These bees are very busy today!

The picture of the busy bees has changed.
Find and circle the 4 things that are different.

Some people catch fish through a hole in the ice.

The picture looks different now. Find and circle the
4 things that have changed.

Luis is getting ready to throw the football
to his teammate.

Now look at the picture of Luis. Find 5 things that have changed and circle them.

These penguins are enjoying some winter fun.

There are 4 things different in the picture.
Can you find and circle all of them?

This mouse and its friends have found
something tasty to eat!

Look carefully at the picture and circle the
5 things that have changed.

23

Rebecca loves to jump rope, especially
outdoors on a nice day.

Now circle the 4 things that have
changed in the picture.

Albert can't wait to taste his cool treat!

What's this? The picture is different! Circle the
5 things that have changed.

Whee! Jack and Molly are taking turns on the slide.

If you look carefully, you will find 3 things that
are different in the picture. Circle them all.

Tiger and Polly are visiting this pretty flower.

The picture has changed. Find and circle the
4 things that are different.

31

Kevin and his dog, Muffin, are enjoying
a bike ride through the park.

The picture looks the same, but 4 things are different. Find and circle them.

Here is a picture of trained seals
performing at the circus.

There are 4 things different in the picture.
Can you find and circle them?

The rooster crows early in the morning
and wakes everyone on the farm.

Circle the 3 things in the picture that make it
different from the one opposite.

Clancy is not ready to go to bed just yet.
He still wants to play!

This picture of Clancy is different from the other one. Circle the 5 things that have changed.

These garden friends get together
every morning at the big log.

Now look at the picture. Find and circle the
4 things that are different.

41

The camel and the snake greet
each other in the desert.

Find the 4 things that are different in this
desert picture and circle them.

Katie practices playing her violin
every day during music class.

This picture is not the same as the one opposite.
Find and circle the 5 things that are different.

These birds gather each day on the
poles to chatter away.

Find and circle the 4 things that have
changed in the picture.

Scrub-a-dub-dub! Michael is having fun in the tub!

Look carefully at the picture of Michael and circle the
4 things that have changed.

49

This duck wants to join its friends in the pond.

Can you find and circle the 5 things that have
changed in the picture?

51

The turtle and the fish are ready for
a swim with the mermaid.

Now look at the picture, and you will find that
5 things have changed. Circle them all.

The giraffe tells a story to its friends.

This picture of the giraffe and its friends has changed. Find
and circle the 4 things that are different.

Maggie makes sure that the plants in
her garden get enough water.

Find and circle the 4 things in the picture that make it different from the other one.

Solutions

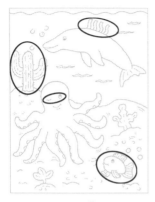

page 5

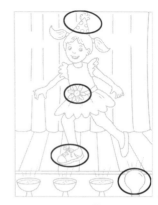

page 7

page 9

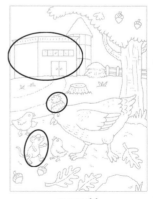

page 11

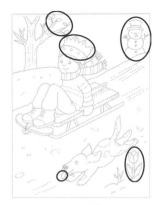

page 13

page 15

page 17

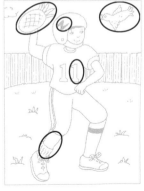

page 19

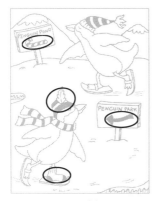

page 21

page 23

page 25

page 27

page 29

page 31

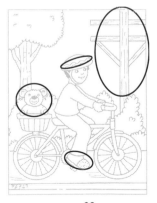

page 33

page 35

page 37

page 39

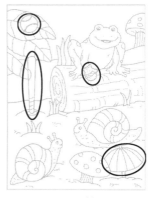

page 41

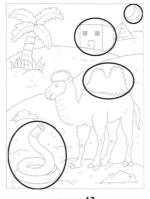

page 43

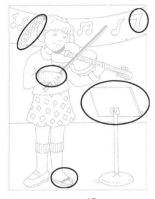

page 45

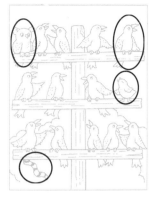

page 47

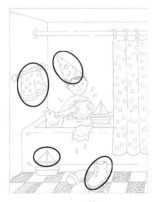

page 49

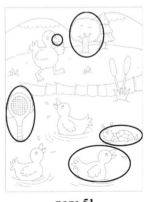

page 51

page 53

page 55

page 57